MANCUNIA

MANCUNIA

Michael Symmons Roberts

CAPE POETRY

1 3 5 7 9 10 8 6 4 2

Jonathan Cape, an imprint of Vintage,
20 Vauxhall Bridge Road,
London SW1V 2SA

Jonathan Cape is part of the Penguin Random House group of companies
whose addresses can be found at global.penguinrandomhouse.com

Penguin
Random House
UK

First published by Jonathan Cape in 2017

penguin.co.uk/vintage

A CIP catalogue record for this book is available
from the British Library

ISBN 9781911214298

Typeset in 11/13 pt Bembo by Jouve (UK), Milton Keynes
Printed and bound in Great Britain by TJ International Ltd, Padstow, Cornwall

Penguin Random House is committed to a sustainable future for
our business, our readers and our planet. This book is made
from Forest Stewardship Council® certified paper.

A map of the world that does not include Utopia is not worth even glancing at.

Oscar Wilde

. . . once went further and saw Manchester, / And once the sea, that blue end of the world.

Elizabeth Barrett Browning, *Aurora Leigh*

What a world it represented – cotton and shipping and commerce, the like of which we shall never see again. It's a wonder they didn't use gold bars instead of bricks and stone.

Beryl Bainbridge

Six thousand years in the Sahara looks like six months in Manchester.

Tom Stoppard

CONTENTS

These poems were completed before the attack at the Manchester Arena on 22 May 2017, but this book is dedicated to the memory of the victims, and to those Mancunians and others who came to offer help and support on that night.

I SHAKE OUT MY COAT

because I cannot sleep and this unsteady
moon has lured me out with promises
to light one final act for me.

Filthy sky-black pea-coat,
I shrug it from my shoulders, grip the collar,
and begin to shake it out.

The stars cannot give second thought
to such a slight shift in the world's array,
but still they flinch with each down-draught.

The backyard breeze, coaxed into mimicry,
awakens fallen leaves from cherries, acers,
laurels, limes, a silvered cloud of tree,

a crack of pylons at the edge of town.
Within an hour, it will be lifting flags
in empty cities you and I have never seen.

I curse myself for waiting days to do this,
given all the places we have been
– turbid rivers, search-lit walls,

dry fields sown with thorns and mines –
no wonder it shakes out so many
splinters, dog-hairs, baggage-tags, such rain.

And given all those half-forgotten places,
it is scant surprise that – *look!* –
my cloth, unfurled, is twice the size.

I had no sense it was so bunched and hemmed,
but now it opens into trench coat, cloak,
black wedding-train, tarpaulin, tent,

and still the dross flies from its folds.
I am a vignette: *man-in-silent-yard-sees-light,*
or *sings-of-where-he's-been-and-what-he-almost-knows.*

O moon, have a heart, my arms are agony,
I cannot stop for fear that when I do,
my old coat will no longer be a fit for me.

GREAT NORTHERN DIVER

Mancunia at night looks like embers from above,
but hold the dive and it reassembles, cools,
coalesces into districts, flyovers, a motherboard,

now stadiums like unblinking eyes,
car lots set out as piano keys, parks with lake wounds,
counter-flow of arteries in red and white,

the bass clef curves of cul de sacs
in outlying estates, then factories with starting guns
of smoke that sting and make you squint,

now you can pick out individual cars, nags' heads
down in dark fields, glow of dressed shop windows,
drunks on their tightrope walk home,

black poplars' ragged tops, roof tiles, kerbstones,
air that drops from ice to cloud to everything a city
cooks at once until the road meets you

face-to-face, down and under, slower, denser
and the clay arrests you, holds you as a pulse for good,
so what keeps this city alive is you.

ON YOUR BIRTHDAY

I give you the Northern Quarter in full vamp,
its post-drizzle glory, sun an arc lamp

on that mural of a blue-tit, vast and antic,
with bindweed blooms like blast-holes in old brick.

Spiralling above this massive passerine,
painted candles rise towards some heaven.

I thought how you would hate that twist,
since you dismiss the promise of all worlds but this,

how you would sooner have your cold cadaver
thrown into a skip than warrant any hope of a hereafter.

The street-cleaners are out in force,
steam from Northern Tea Power frosts its glass,

vintage frock stores shake their racks for moths.
The last payphone on Newton Street rings out,

and picking through the gutter at your feet
a blackbird holds the same trill on repeat.

This is no epiphany, but so close-up,
such is the soft density of darkness on its nap

that like an inverse star it could pull everyone,
the whole unrescued world through to oblivion.

If there is another place, another chapter,
I suggest this Ancoats skylark is its harbinger.

But then you pick it up and show how light it is,
its air sacs and its fluted bones: *it flies.*

ACTAEON

Between back-to-backs along the alleys
he lifts wrung-out sheets
and shirts hung up to dry,
in search of a repeat

glimpse of a goddess out to get
a tan. Meantime, her right-hand-woman
uses his old sweat-soaked gym vest
as gift-wrap for a T-bone,

thus reprogramming his own stray
pack of pit bulls, staffies, akitas,
to see their master as their prey.
They do. So said the stars.

RHYME OF A MERCHANT MARINER

I know exactly how you feel:
you're like some drunken bluebottle

which wakes from winter's bite not just alive
but in the tropics, and cannot believe

that this is real, such paradise,
with plates of fruit and meat, you buzz

from room to room and this
becomes complete for you, a universe.

How could you know
that just beyond that picture window

lies a world of barren fields and ice.
That's you, a blowfly trapped inside a house.

God love you, you have not a clue
what *world* might mean. I do.

I plied the merchant lines with beet,
but sugar magnates forced me out.

I changed my tack, went north, worked harder,
struck an iceberg, *yadda, yadda* . . .

Drifted to an island, swam ashore,
learned their lingo and their lore,

my face the only foreign land they knew.
You want another drink? I think you do.

I missed my wife and kids back home,
they gave me six wives - *when in Rome* . . .

I stayed a year, then tides turned bad.
Long story, a cantankerous bird.

One shot, and I lost everything:
the house, the status – I was king.

They gave me a boat and cast me out.
Got home to find my wife with my first mate.

So ever since, those wild north shores
have been my lodestar, and they could be yours.

The gods are on your side tonight,
this dive, this hour, my table, why the fates

have chosen you is theirs to know
but now you're here that picture window

cannot con you any more,
a blowfly knows that every measure

of contentment rests on prejudice,
the shortest day in one place

is the longest day elsewhere.
So, barfly, I tender you this brochure.

Open it and read if you have ever
(*who has not?*) promised a lover

you will treat them to a toe-hold
in the other, to own a piece of stone-cold

real estate in what I call *Utopia*,
and this is cut right to the bone, this offer,

one night only. Okay, it's a fire sale,
I can't shift these final parcels,

everyone wants perfect now,
so what's an honest hustler meant to do?

I'll tell you what, I'll throw the beak in free.
Here, I wear it like a rosary.

You like it? It's my lucky charm.
Once bad, now good, it's done its harm.

Reminds me of a mussel shell
or shepherd's whistle. Blow it, and the north pole

answers back in tones too
high for us. Your dog will love you.

THE PARTY WALL

'Something there is that doesn't love a wall'

Robert Frost

What divides us? Language,
habit, shyness, levee, breeze-block,
rockwool, horsehair, plaster, lath . . .

From now on, regard yourself joint
owner of a whole wall, not sole owner
of the half that bears your wallpaper.

Rest your ear against the cold
and eavesdrop on the dark interstice
separating your domain from theirs.

That sheet of stillness held between
the bricks is neither in nor out,
no fixed abode, a no-man's-land

of silverfish and woodlice, cross-hatch
of cables and the sharp ends of nails,
neither one world nor the next,

a space where all your cries and songs
crossfade with theirs – where
you and your co-owner harmonise.

From now, like Pyramus and Thisbe,
see cracks as conduits for words of love,
for breath, for perfume. Press your lips

against the rictus in the plaster,
cross the threshold with a whisper,
answer now: *who is my neighbour?*

COD WITH THE VOICE OF A CANTOR

Still we send the trawlers out, although no one alive
has heard the song, and no one dead will tell.

Boat after boat hauls back, and captains hold
their silent ground on decks of gasping contraband

to listen for a note, a tentative first 'O'
among the mottled greens, the sand-brown, lobster blue.

So with fathometers we scan the north Atlantic
in the hope of anthems welled-up in the liver

of this loose bag of fish, that begs to be in batter,
fillet it as if to find the staves and dots are written through.

Around the world tonight, these Arctic steels are fried
and served in last night's newspapers

and even those who do not know the urban myth
will hesitate a moment, wood-fork poised,

as sirens stop, a tram freewheels, car alarms hold back
mid-flash before the prongs go in.

A silent grace, this superstitious pause, which goes
unquestioned, as if from these locked maws

a note may rise, the one we need to hear,
the sound of seas retreating, song that summoned

life from souped-up slime to all of this,
in truth, its maker's voice, ventriloquising

through a dead cod on your plate,
the beauty of its timbre as dark, opaque and full

as this fish-eye, as fathomless, and yet within a day
so misremembered that its one-chance listener

is cast out under city lights, thrown out of bar after bar,
driven to despair by that half-forgotten song,

hanging out in fish-and-chip shops, shushing customers,
his ear pressed to the hot, lit glass.

LOVE SONG ON A LOOP

So help me, I feel it, true enough,
but there is nothing,
not one thing I could say
that would hold its value in these times.

If I told you I love you,
then tomorrow a cache of new
ballads of truer love may come to light
and devalue its currency,

or prove that it was nothing more
than traps set by your DNA,
a legacy as dry as all the ash, hair, dust
that gathers under floorboards.

And so this song undoes itself,
unwinding into gibberish.
Nonetheless, it started
true enough, I feel it, so help me.

SUPERINTENDENT OF PUBLIC SPECTACLES

Even he, on slow afternoons
as he files his reports on tuneless buskers,
living statues caught out breathing,
street magicians sent to re-learn their trade
because too many ladies have been found,

even he will let his gaze wander through
his office window out across the roof-scape,
where a mongrel barks on a balcony,
where a nurse hands in her notice,
sick of the sick. She strides out past

those die-hard smokers on the steps,
wheeling their drip-rigs, on their last legs.
Even he (who understands spectacle,
who knows how it can seize the attention
so an audience forgets its future)

can imagine this consummate age,
this commonwealth, all lost except a single square
of woven glass-fibre from a transistor radio,
washed up on a distant shore,
with the ghost of a circuit mapped onto it.

The left edge of our vitrine is the downslope of a breast-shaped sandstone wall and that spear-bearing boy note at his feet this predator with teeth brigand wears a pair of snakeskin boots bought from a boutique owned above whose perfect hair hangs an experimental aeroplane designed by ladder tending to the first computer watching policewomen kissing at the schoolkids spin-bowling a clockwork orange being painted by the old been now note the author of *Condition of the Working Class in England* how the world was on the skew and there his old pal sits in Chetham's live on blackened chimneys *yes this see-through box is graphene-strong* so believable) is waiting for the world-famous nightclub to open its doors the bastille almost drowning out the shouts of *Judas* as a tambourine man my parents met now eyes down and you catch the poor victims of by dockland cranes *the real ones seized by rust now* and rows of clerks at late soup dinner stirred with his baton by the maestro still in tails while the novelist who marked out *North and South* for us here strolling in a up of cotton fibres cut with silk and snow-like spits of paper ever falling who form cross-species packs in order to survive towards the right edge blank unwritten I can fix for you to come in here last thing when all the

DIORAMA

rise and on its fall a Roman fort *Mancunium* depicted by this fearsome
around a Celtic neck is wolf not whippet and beneath his smock the
by that lad there the world's first rock-star footballer *yes they are all wax*
a philosopher whose upturned eyes are met by that code-cracker on his
Pride Parade now file along past mills and mills and mills the ragged
boy in a mac and cap who draws in more dogs than there could have
being led through slums by his Irish lover she who *really* showed him
Library distracted from his manifesto by our peppered moths evolved to
now you hear a snatch of song that queue of people (far too long to be
and halfway down the line you clock a noble suffragette plotting to storm
plugs in up the road next door to Tootal Textiles where (a personal aside)
Peterloo with cavalry long gone attended by their loved ones overlooked
desks inscribing bills of lading and now *shhhh* you hear the simmer of a
beyond his kitchen flows the Irwell and its banks are being walked by
bid to take the air but there is little left for her to take just smoke made
from the Arndale bomb much to the terror of the animals at Belle Vue
of the case where our blizzard pixillates and all turns sandstorm isabelline
crowds have cleared although the weight of it can be too much to bear.

BLOOD-LINES

We honour our ancestors by becoming them,
our every song a tribute act.
How better could we thank them

than to take on the snub of a nose,
the slant of a jaw, the way
we hang our heads when cowed.

Even when we dress to differ
it is just a costume, nobody is fooled,
the old utopians live in us still.

Give in to it, you find your tongue
will soon shape a thought in
some long-scrambled lingua franca.

And every mirror, every shop window
you pass becomes an echo chamber
with a single diamond

at the far end of its telescopic tunnel,
unbreakable and blind.

MANUKA

Deliver us from blood, O God,
for it lacks the viscosity to hold us up now,
the sweetness to warm us on days like these.

We are done with its showy scarlet
each time it meets a nick or slit, its headlong
dash through us, the blue badge it leaves where

we are struck. Give us instead honey,
let us wander through the film-sets of this city
as serene as manatees, generous with our time,

our words of hope full-weighed
and waited for, our every fight or fall distracted
into dance as slow as reef-fish and as bright.

SELF-PORTRAIT WITH DOG

It was the same one every time,
different guises when demanded by a role,
but the same mutt hunting on cave walls,
in wide-shots of B-movie hick towns,

barking at a stray cat out of shot,
in Roman mosaics, Flemish paintings,
coats of arms and porcelain figurines,
posed lovingly to heel and looking out.

It was the same dog that howled offstage
in countless poems set at night,
or lay beside a deathbed, loyal and quiet,
or killed a man in atavistic rage.

We worked him hard, from walk-on parts
in myths to slope-off parts in novels,
all to take a measure to ourselves,
of faith, of duty, the temper of our feral hearts.

So I set out to hunt for him.
I wanted him as currency, to pay my way across
from this tame world to wilderness,
and he, as go-between, could break that line.

A dirt-track, off a slip road, off a byway – lost.
More lost than ever, close to home.
Low solstice sun made bare trees bloom,
I left the car and walked into a copse.

And there he stood, afraid of me but sure
this was his ground, I called him
by his many names. He answered none of them.
I wanted him to step into my story,

but he crouched, gave teeth, drew back,
body raked and scant, would not be caught.
We have him trapped here between is and ought,
still dutiful, still longing for the work.

SOLILOQUY OF THE INNER EMIGRÉ

The authorities asked us to call at noon,
to test their new helpline.
No one was available to answer our questions.

I kept the line open just in case,
held the phone to my ear all afternoon,
until its ringtone was my metronome.

Devolution is a constant process:
each week I secede another stage,
ratchet back and back

from every bloc until I am a law
unto myself. It is a mystery
to me why the warm summer core

of this city is so silent tonight.
Maybe everyone has run off to the woods
to watch our gods and goddesses

disport themselves, now it's a free-for-all.
But there is live news on TV, quiet bars
ravenous for custom, empty trams on time –

the pointless daily liturgies continue.
I dare not lift the blinds to look.
But my ringtone prays for me unceasingly.

I have become an anchorite.
I put the phone on speaker to rest my arm.
Tomorrow I withdraw into a single room.

This is an elegy whichever way I spin it,
to call to mind a city without you in it.

MY FATHER'S DEATH

I don't believe in omens,
but that wedding bowl in smithereens,
then the starling in our hallway
whose fear sent the dog into a fury,

then those cast-in-blue recurrent dreams
in which he visits me and seems
aware of some unspoken threat
from which I wake in dread, *and yet,*

and yet he is still here, *thank God.* Am I
dry-running for that day,
as if to preview loss might stem its force,
and so he goes, and goes, and goes?

I need to break its hold.
I set a trap, an apple pursed with mould,
heavy with its sick perfume:
open window, north-facing room.

I sit in wait and watch it land:
my father's death, close up, new-spawned
or rather, hatched,
so purposeful in dreams, now, watched,

can barely hold its line in air,
I speak out loud a childhood prayer
I only half-believe
and on the *s* of *save*

it flutters to my hand and look,
its iridescent jet, its wings of black lacework,
the hidden kernel of a rose,
a gothic wind-up toy. *So close.*

COORDINATOR OF MISREADINGS

I had my head down,
washing my face from the midday sweat,
when a bird flew over the skylight

giving out an instant of darkness,
and I knew then that nothing
would ever be the same,

that blood-letting would start,
then looting, the loosening of bonds
between us all, until in weeks

we would be picking over
ash-mounds, lifting broken roof-tiles
to see if we could find

that precious photograph or letter,
and we would never be sure
if the bird had been warning or delivering.

But when I went downstairs
onto the street, nothing had changed,
the fruit-stalls ripe and full,

a spill of nothing more than cola
from a half-drunk bottle,
and that harbinger, a herring gull,

jabbing at a rolled up newspaper
holding a still warm fillet of fish.
Somebody has to have these fears,

to misconstrue each sign.
How else can we ward it off,
that end they have in mind for us?

MANCHURIA

Where the Great Steppe falters
into forests, trips on bare roots
as it slows, then cuts its feet
on jagged mountain ranges,

a box (weather-beaten but intact)
sent by his overseas twin
arrives at a doorman's desk
in an empty condominium.

The customs declaration says:
one peppered moth, one phial of Irwell water,
the rest illegible. It weighs no less
than a head with a big idea in it.

TIGHTROPE SONG

'Fast I stood / whose falling could have felled them all'

Dream of the Rood

Not a noose or a net, no hawser of hemp,
not coiled in a boatyard's oil and damp,

the job they gave me was to bear
the weight of a man as he walked through the air,

the flight of a god who would dance on my back.
So they play me out from bank to bank,

east to west like a hand-drawn line,
like a fine-nibbed scratch on a painted scene

of fly-boats, quack-stalls, string quartets,
swimmers, peddlers, drunks, and yet . . .

All twenty thousand pairs of eyes
are drawn to me, where world divides.

Above me: ether, angels, sun,
too bright to look for long. Then down,

below me: surface-stippling flies,
then fish, then mud, then rock, then fire.

I steel myself for the heft of a man,
He plants his right foot, left, then runs

full-tilt, and many – to their shame –
watch him, but not me holding him,

and think this is his miracle
– his Galilee – to risk a fall

not just through deeps, but out of sky,
and yet the conjurer is me:

I hold him slack, I hold him tight,
I sway and dip to meet his weight.

He goes again with a man on his back,
he stands halfway and fries a steak,

he offers a fee for the loan of a child,
and mothers queue for their sons to be held

as if, once crossed from land to land,
no border or threshold could ever stand,

as if to be borne through emptiness
is a charm against limit, a get-out clause

from jail cells, cotton mills, dust-to-dust,
because if this man is able to trust

his life and theirs to a fibrous twist,
then those he carries must be blessed.

So this prince of the air climbs down from me,
to carve his name on an ancient tree,

and the crowd goes wild for a touch of his hand,
a gift from the heavens to dull, dry land.

They cut me down and haul me in
like a corn-coloured eel from a slow, deep swim,

then hang me up on a bough to dry
beneath an undivided sky.

GALLERY OF DELETED PORTRAITS

You must have known they were not lost,
those countless rows of photographs
deleted because of a half-blink,
some accidental grimace,
but among them is this treasure:
you in a split-second ecstasy

caught at the apex with eyelids full shut
despite the midday dazzle and rush
of a great metropolis behind you:
street-vendors I can almost hear,
exhaust fumes I can almost smell.
You stand in full repose.

Behind you, a police car holds its roof-light still
like it's delivering a blue curaçao
to some plutocrat who will not wait.
A kebab-vendor in mid-shout
has won the attention of a terrier
walked by a girl whose back-story is safe

inside her battered, unseasonal coat,
and everyone is hustling,
for eye contact, for a proximate brush
with each other's contactless cards, but for you,
this is your time to be the shuttle pin
that holds us all together.

The world is neither terrible nor good,
because to say so would require
a working knowledge of another world
to make comparison,
yet here you are at peace in it,
complicit and complete.

BAREFOOT IN MANCUNIA

So proud is he of his unofficial duty
that he cuts, stitches, dyes

a uniform befitting the role
of *postman-to-the-places-no-one-else-will-go*,

but does not run to boots,
so he walks the ill-lit city streets

on rain and coins and shattered glass,
until they print through the soles of his feet.

Only by such raw connection
can he hold the grid in muscle-memory:

how streets break onto one another,
then another, until wasteland.

Mail-rates rise in mid-life,
then taper to a tail of bills and birthdays.

His judgement calls are many:
when to speak, when listen,

how to hand over a red letter,
when to withhold and when to deliver.

BARFLY

Why must the dead sing to us all night,
crooning through countless speakers
for their impossible desires and regrets?

It's not just their voices, they come complete
with ghost-orchestras, and though I know
in truth they are colossal in their silence,

it's hard not to feel pestered by their songs.
Who are the dead? asks a barfly, balanced on my glass.
Is that phrase not as empty as 'the lovers', or 'the lost'?

I try to swat him away,
but his countless eyes are locked on mine,
and he has urgent messages for me.

Our forebears, says the fly, *speak through musak
and repeat each song until we heed their warnings
but we are such poor listeners,*

*caught up in the detail of our work,
the mysteries of money, futures, that we talk over
these siren voices even as they try to save us.*

No sooner has he spoken than the fly
drops dead into my scotch between a pair of icebergs.
I pluck him from the amber ocean,

place him on a coaster to dry out,
and he is intricate, delicate, so sweetly made,
as if cut from coal and utterly at peace.

WHAT'S YOURS IS MINE

'Doors which yield to a touch of the hand . . . permit anyone to enter.'

Thomas More, *Utopia*

It was our game, to drive at night into their city,
scan the streets, choose a house at random,
stroll in mid-evening as the householders
were finishing, say, a birthday dinner.
We watched them look up, terrified but mute.

We picked lamb off their plates, emptied their glasses
then ran upstairs, threw open drawers,
tried on jackets, fingered through their journals,
pocketed the odd keepsake – scarf, set of car keys,
half-read book, a piece of underwear for shame.

We tried to get a rise from them by breakage:
a cabinet of crystal cups, statuettes of local gods,
but they were patient in their sad-masks.
Such acquiescence, you knew they saw you straight,
and even so would give you everything.

Our only rule: we never touched them.
Save one time I saw a blue heart-shaped soap
clutched in a woman's hand and something in her
would not give it up to me for all the world.
I have it somewhere. Let me find it.

MANCUNIAN MISERERE

As I walk west on Cross Street have mercy on me, O God,
for the cold of my fingers, the clam of my palms,
for the knots I have tied in my tongue and for their undoing,
for my constancy of inattention, for my inner tension and its ills,
for the fact that the undersides of leaves (my mother told me)
are blown visible before a storm but I forget to look,
for the unlearned lore that rain when it runs unhindered
in a gutter will still trouble itself into opacity, for the cities
– rich, exotic, gifted – of my days that I have sacked, abandoned,
given up for the price of a light, my hands cupped in case
you try to blow it out, for thinking you would waste your
    breath on me,
for fearing you may not, for the coin-jar I save for a deluge,
for the wide berth I gave that man-cocoon asleep on the steps
of a new-closed bank where once I queued to find my balance,
for the stars I thank, for the losses I adjust, for the cost
have mercy, let the seas hold themselves, let the streets dry out
and flood instead the cambers, ventricles, capillaries of me,
prise my teeth apart O God that I might learn to praise.

TERRA PERICOLOSA

The only reason we let gardens be lost
is for the joy of finding them again.

Take a slant path through the planners' grid,
the un-policed sectors of the city

where the wireframe gets sketchy,
and at the back of a hoarding which reads

what's mine is yours discover this:
a paradise of ordered beds, fountains, pergolas,

clearly tended, but for no one's use,
in the same way we lose memories

until with the shock of a tune or a scent
your mind contrives to bring back

the face of someone you once loved
as vivid and familiar as the mirror,

and you catch yourself off guard,
button up your coat and walk away,

vow never to speak of this garden again.

MASTER OF LIGHTING SMALL DETAILS

Raise a glass you lonely souls,
to the master of lighting small details,

or mistress, more likely, either way
the sun still does her work as if to an itinerary:

countless spotlit points – a discarded can,
frost-blown brick – such secret signs,

each lit for one and one alone to see,
they read: *this is your desire path, follow me.*

Today my route is waymarked as it is
each day, a painstaking, pig-headed, pointless

act because that path was long ago
not taken, and that choice is why this cameo

poem frames me, held forever glass on lip,
since early doors I gave today the slip,

to spend my lunch-hour in a bar
drinking mild to toast the way things are

and might have been, if I had just . . .
And since there's no one left I fully trust

to bear my secrets through the days and nights
I find my company of one feels right.

Yet all those miles away some clutch
of thistles catches midday sun with such

rare glory that a traveller through
that field may stop to take it in as though

the glimpse of it was meant for him,
and walk my path as it were his own.

But scrub all this. If subtle light-effects
are all this world can do to mark a loss

then I will sit and stare into my glass
until the swirl of dark and head resolves.

THE COLD

Despite this blizzard, or because of it,
the dog wants letting out. In summer she was white,

but now she can't compete. Instead,
she starts to eat it off what was the road,

as if by this brute method she can free us.
Outgunned, outnumbered, she looks up at the geese

in their *greater-than* formation cutting low over
the roofs, and I, at this half-opened door

– dressed for an inner life, facing an outer –
know neither one thing nor the other.

Sky is blank, and endless blank, but that was never
the place to find a cure for this cold fever.

If prayers are heard, as I believe they are,
then they are heard here without fear or favour,

and the answers must be here too, solid and sure.
Across the road, swaddled, my neighbour

the retired accountant scrapes and shovels
out beyond his drive into the street, and still it falls.

I try to reckon up if I should go to him,
if the rate of two digging could win us this game,

or if we should give in to it, wait for the melt.
God of the snows, I know this silence is my fault,

I have kept your voice too distant, hard to pick out
from the freight trains, cold calls, backchat,

when I should feel your breath against my cheek,
words so clear that I could not mistake

your answers for my own. So here, a prayer
for the frostbitten feet of Captain Oates, whose Terra Nova

ended in a walk off the edge of the earth,
for the hands of Francis Bacon, who met death

while trying to stuff a fowl with ice,
for the deep-sounded lungs of Louis MacNeice,

who caught his in a cave recording echoes,
for the kicked-out, street-sleepers, hawkers and strays,

for the eyes of a driver hunched over his wheel,
for the guts, lungs, lights that make us real,

I stare into the beautiful nil, winter's empyrean,
then scrap that prayer and start again.

OFF GREAT ANCOATS STREET

Nobody offers to help him,
the man who was shot in the leg,
who drags himself through city parks,
shopping malls, across the wastes
of hollowed-out estates.

He has come to warn us,
has broken free from your TV screen.
A freak reconstellation of pixels
has marooned him miles from his
sacked desert citadel.

And you want to ask
about the blood-loss, how to stem it,
so you rip the shirt off your back
to make a ligature,
then look up and he's vanished.

So many times he does this,
now it's only foreigners like you
who fall for him. His wound is real,
as is his battledress,
but we have heard it all before.

He could get stitched,
like the rest of us, cover it with clothes,
disguise the lag in his step.
He could tell you a joke,
ask for a light, give you directions.

Instead he abandons you
half-naked on a windswept square,
your shirt twisted like a rag,
while in a box-room streets away
a hopeless drummer tries a break.

THE VALUE OF NOTHING

Two white dogs tear into each other
in a sunlit square, over nothing more

than a marbled twist of gristle
from a bin-raid. Fur red-spittled

as they turn from pets to curs,
their prize of meat is nothing, or a cipher

for pure nothing, a McGuffin
to be spat into the gutter when it's won.

A crowd forms. Men make bets
which none intends to pay. Now let

me lead you from this maelstrom
to a backstreet cafe. Sit down.

No, here, by that picture of the sea
at Rimini. In that same seat a refugee

who fled the noose for heresy
once lingered with his malady

– a woman he loved more than anything –
and in his old silk waistcoat was a ring

once worn by a czarina, silver band
with amethyst, clouded in his hand.

He closed his fist on it, dinner after dinner
at this table, holding back for fear

she would say no, so when at last
he offered it, the worst

had happened – cavers in Brazil,
prospectors in China had struck purple,

so he bought her a crown jewel
and left her with a Christmas bauble.

Except, of course, it did not matter.
They left in love, ignored the tattered

mutt that sloped past with its tail down.
This all took place before you were born.

You ask about his heresy? No one knows.
They say his people met in shadows,

used a simple rite involving ice and oils,
believed their bodies were suits for their souls.

My hunch is that their true fault lay
in thinking they could change their destiny

with amethysts as amulets, deep Russian,
dark as plum-blood, worth a fortune.

DUMB SHOW

I do remember one last thing:
some troupers in a camper van,
who never tried to speak or sing,
but toured the city with a plan

to win us over via mime,
one masked as *Virtue*, one as *Vice*,
or one as *Law* and one as *Crime*.

I wish now we had paid more heed.
I do recall the *Virtue* girl
wore a string of purple beads.

Their van had foreign number-plates.
It was summer, we were young,
they were dumb, knew everything.
Lost on us, and far too late.

PEACEMAKER

'Such civil war is in my love and hate'

Shakespeare, *Sonnet 35*

To put this civil war to bed at last,
I step offstage, watch sex scenes from the wings,
our lives played out by better-looking cast,
forbidden lovers pocketing their rings.

It's safe out here, beyond the sonnet's frame,
(though I can mouth the words before they're said)
my love as metadrama: burlesque games,
a tragedy where no one winds up dead.

But as my hapless actor shouts the odds,
hands shaking as they hold your sobbing face,
it sounds like melodrama, from the gods –
who cares who is betrayed and who betrays?

I lay the ceasefire treaties out to sign:
a caveat, a sub-clause, more delays.
Meanwhile, on stage, he busks a fifteenth line.

DEMETRIUS TO THE AUDIENCE

Look at me, framed by the safety curtain.
Those offended by full-frontal nakedness
may leave the theatre now, but no returns.

Remember, when the curtain rose,
how I disdained that woman, tried to shake her off,
then caught the fluence and was lost?

Now our play is done, I stand before you,
shrunk and shivering as a half-drowned cat.
To the sceptics I say: does this do

the trick? Do you see me in another light?
Where could I hide a lie in here?
A smuggler of roles, drug mule at an airport?

Will you demand a scan? Cavity search?
You have the naked facts, embodied here by mine.
So stare. But as you stare, consider

that when every trace of fakery is gone,
it's still a desperate mystery to you *and me*,
how this stripped wretch, a man,

is left here gasping like a tide-torn fish.
My every cell in thrall to her. I'm sick.
You think I'm still in role? I wish.

I want to face you without artifice – *defenceless*
I would flay myself in front of you if it
would help me prove my case.

But even flensed would not ring true
for those determined to see guile
where there is none, a feint in skin, an after-show.

I knew that the dismantling of skies,
enchanted forests, glades and mirror pools
would not convince you if the witness of your eyes

said *man-in-costume*, so I broke the spell:
house-lights up and all revealed as painted flats,
racks of lights, seats for sale.

All gone, except this stripped wretch, yes a man,
this sacred flesh, enchanted piece of meat.
Your silence chills me. I must get my clothes on.

THE FUTURE OF BOOKS

Or this: some sci-fi aeon where a drill
draws out a deep core sample,
a candy-stick of sands and clays,
each civilisation – the gist of all its stories –
packed into a slab of sediment.
Our slice has its own distinctive shade and scent
– paper-musk, the dark behind bookshelves –
but it so mystifies our future selves
they fry it like black pudding, a salt and bitter
jus of atlas, sonnet, gossip, scripture.
Text is long gone, cut loose in virtual vaults
with mislaid passcodes. Think of bottles
on a cyber-tide, never breaking shore,
bearing love letters for strangers.

An insomniac tunes in to a split
in the guttering where steady drip–drips
stain the wall and moss marks it.

That's how it starts. Then she summons
water with a chant like a nursery rhyme
and orchestrates its fall,

swells the veins of mountain streams,
strums the high wires between pylons,
lays it low in crowded city squares,

but if anyone should think
that she is gathering it to hoard it,
let it be known she calls it down through

limestone, gritstone, shafts,
through leaf-clogged pipes on house-walls,
simply for the fall's polyphony.

Don't define her by her sleeplessness,
this woman has known and given love,
how else could she do this?

The sun through blinds has marked up
staves across her bed. She lies in them,
and outside, we all run for cover.

IN PARADISUM

Three thousand refugee children arrive in our city,
or rather, camp on flood-plains by the ship canal,
or rather, have no tents, so sit down
among thistles and dock and nettles,
on rain-hammered concrete,
hang their backpacks on spars of rusted iron
up from the earth like ribs of giants disinterred.
Soon they make a tarpaulin village.

Unaccompanied, three thousand refugee children
are leaderless, and though we dare not think
of what they hold inside their heads
they look for all the world like any kids
with their ball-games and fights and gangs.
Not that we know how three thousand refugee children
should behave, but we will know when we see it.
We slow our cars past them as a mark of respect,

and three thousand refugee children
return that nobility by looking back at us,
as if in a slow-motion tracking shot at the end
of a film when the train sets off to rescue or deport,
and some are aboard but some are not. Trust us,
we will determine what three thousand refugee children
need and give it to them. Our best minds are on it,
and will not sleep until the strategy is clear.

In the meantime, we have to go to work.
We have to tend to the numbers, to ensure
we keep unrestricted funds from restricted funds,
unprotected assets from protected assets.
We have to maintain the beauty of our public spaces,
to live as fully as we can in the present moment,

because that is what three thousand refugee children
long for, and to lose it is to let them down.

Believe us, we have tried to find interpreters,
but three thousand refugee children speak
a dialect of a dialect of a long-lost tongue
beyond the ears of our philologists.
Some nights, we leave a window open
to listen for the cries of three thousand refugee children,
in the hope that a cry might unlock it for us,
or unlock something inside us.

Other nights we lie awake and try to separate
them in our minds, to give them names,
so the one in the Brazil shirt becomes *Paulo*,
and the one in the blue smock his cousin *Lily*,
and their parents worked a dry field in the hills,
and their grandparents repaired shoes
and kept an unwritten repository of stories
to pass on to three thousand refugee children.

And their days in the homeland, though spare,
though lean, were on the whole benign
until those flares on the horizon grew closer,
and closer, and came for them.
But no sooner, in the ease of night, have we
begun to picture them, than some fox in a bin
breaks the trance and *Lily* and *Paulo* snap back
into three thousand refugee children.

TERRA INCOGNITA

A border is a border,
so knowing well the score
I was divesting myself from miles out,
on trains, on buses, boats,
then on foot through the woods,

I'm thinking: wipe off
all that camo paint,
cut up all your credit cards,
deactivate your passcodes.
unlearn the tongue-twists of dialect.

By the time I reach the gate
I'm like tomorrow's page in a diary.
But the post is unattended:
no guns, no uniforms, no barrier,
in fact no border at all,

just the gatehouse of a mansion, ruined,
tattooed with illegible graffiti,
further in, a village boarded up,
just the idiot left behind,
reciting his full name over and over.

Hours after, we are in a city
without ever having crossed a line,
at least not knowingly.
We dare not open our lips
in case a word gives us away.

They split us up and take us in,
clothe and feed us,
patient for us to reveal ourselves,
but we cannot recall
what it is we have left to reveal.

COURSE OF THE ANYDER

Or, the failure of a river as a metaphor for time,
since it dried up overnight, so

next morning, citizens walked the banks
with ghoulish fascination, but after the first day

when it failed to return they mourned it,
shocked by its nakedness,

this cut-away perspective of a blood vessel
clogged with caramel silt embossed

with goose, duck, heron prints,
a single jackboot, countless empty bottles.

I stand and close my eyes,
try to wish it back in brackish straits where brine

and spring-sweet come together in a stand-off
and a line is held.

I listen for the gulp, the first lip-spittle
swollen, fat, insensate, lost in little swirls,

in pockets of thought
as it swells again below the footbridge,

lags beneath an overhang of turf from a meadow's edge
it has long undercut,

then jack-knifes left and all is chase,
troubled and torpid, surface crazed and poly-vocal,

hairpins right, then left again,
gets slimmer, younger as it rolls.

Except it doesn't come.
This artery, this river *No-Water* has collapsed

into its name, as if some child
had found the source and whispered into it

the meaning of *Anyder*
so it dried into self-consciousness.

MANICHEAN

Before the army comes they send in chefs,
hotfoot from the outskirts in white aprons,
picking milk berries and wire-balls of thorn,
shtumm about their mission and beliefs

but absolute in purpose, *now taste this*,
from griddles on our streets they conjure flavours
unimagined but familiar, drawn from park weed,
roadside verge detritus, essence of *us*.

The more we eat, the less we understand
their strategy - they make no moves,
just tend to us so well it feels like love, leaves us
unsure if we are poisoned or seduced.

THE FLOURISH

Beyond the point where we will care
about the manner of our deaths,
when our eyes are drawn shut,
our toes tagged, plastic sheet pulled up
across our faces, for just one day

our bodies will bloom,
an awakening of genes by the thousand,
a contagion of wound-healing,
a glory, all too late, but no
less astonishing for that.

The genes that shaped us in the womb
are woken too, sparking like a swarm
outstripping winter,
one mayfly fury beyond our deaths,
and then we die again for real.

So tonight, in a city under siege,
we rise like instars from a river,
weightless in hope, to celebrate our lives,
not caring that it took an overwhelming
army to bring us this late grace.

MISS MOLASSES

after Elizabeth Bishop's 'The Man-Moth'

Here, above,
on the wind-cut roofs of Quay House, Dock House, Bridge House,
you can keep a night-long vigil, lie in wait for her, tease out
her subtle call from the sob-songs and bulletins and sirens of
    the city.
Good luck with it. She has a startle-reflex so acute the slightest
hint of you – a cough, smell of mint, the moon caught on a watch-face –
and she's gone, down the glass-faced towers back into the Ship
    Canal,
a ripple the size of a cap in the still waters under the swing bridge.

But when this salt-lass
surfaces – fugitive and rare – in daylight, at the earliest of doors
before the trams spark up, before the breakfast show begins,
she moves between dimensions: a *traceuse* over steel and concrete,
a pulse of light along the fibre-optic cables, a data burst
between, above, within and through the runnels, like a sliver,
    like an elver,
like a half-digital, half-analogue orphan of the old docks,
evolved to live and hunt and thrive in this gotham of the north.

Up the façades,
she feels for the gaps and seams in these towers, slides in
with a shimmy and a flick, and starts her search, on empty desks,
in stacks of paper, backs of sofas. This quest is not borne of spirit,
nor of mind, she has no picture in her head of what she's
    looking for.
Instead, it rises from her bones, as close to her as thirst, as hunger,
drives her up and out from the silted bed of this Salford basin,
an endless longing for the one thing that she's lost.

Then she returns,
empty-handed, empty-hearted, to the solace of unwitnessed waters.
And if you ever wondered where she came from, our best guess is
some mesh of sun, brine and cargo-spill at the mouth of
    the Mersey
where it lips the Irish Sea, an accidental alchemy of salmon smolt
and roach, tobacco, sisal, mangrove bark, cotton seeds and copper,
this all conjured *her*, our shy chimera, and she tracked the
    great ships
inland through such foul water that one fag-end could ignite it all.

Each night she must
rehearse all these, the details of her origins, to try to work out
what she's missing: how she grew lithe and strong beneath
the rusted hulls, the shadows of the dockside cranes, how she fed
on coffee, butter, beeswax from the holds and warehouses,
how a docker saw her slipping out one night, dripping with
    cane syrup,
took it for a brunette sweep of hair and called her *Miss Molasses,*
gave birth to the myth of the Salford mermaid and her song.

If you catch her,
run a flashlight over her scales, see the cross-hatch of scratches
    and wounds
from her desperate climbs and leaps. What does she want from us?
Take a microphone and hold it to her lips, turn up the gain
to try to catch a word on the end of her tongue,
a line or a list or an old lament for the salt she left behind,
in a voice as rich and sweet as sorghum, maple, blackstrap,
    barley malt.
She wants to bear witness, but she needs all your attention.

THE FALL OF UTOPIA

The irony is that the morning before
I had lifted my head to the bathroom mirror

and seen for the first time
that face staring back not as me, but mine.

Then as the water wasted in the bowl,
this body I had taken for my soul

plain-eyeballed me and said:
the things I've done for you, you did,

and though you may not buy that old conceit
– soul-as-captain-of-a-bone-ribbed-boat –

it's more than time you took the wheel.
And yet some boat it was, its only sail

was this goose-tendered skin.
I looked it slowly up and down,

like some sad pilgrim sounding out
a coracle to see if it would bear his weight,

and through the window I could hear
not bird-choirs from each English shire

but one sick blackbird's stark distress-call
which kept on and on, until

my ears, in need of song, picked out
a tune in it, and like a harbour pilot

I resolved to steer this vessel made of grief
through latticeworks of rocks and reefs.

TERRA NULLIUS

There is a victory parade moving through the city,
in dress-down garb to look like us,
in its cavalcade of mid-price family sedans,
because the limos, black-lacquered like miso bowls,
are stabled away, the tunics on racks in warehouses
because it is too soon for the trappings of the future.

There is a victory parade moving through the city,
but no one stops to look up, no one checks
in mid-stride, even daytime drinkers in their sop
keep staring down into the glass where one bright bulb
above the bar is circling on the surface.

There is a victory parade moving through the city,
a motorcade with armoured glass.
Our liberators wave to us, they offer eye-contact
to all they pass, but no one takes them up on it.
And this, let it be said, is not some velvet revolution.

There is a victory parade moving through the city.
We do not fear them. Their propaganda is crude,
their speeches dull. But there are shirts to wash,
this coffee will not drink itself, nor will
the beds self-make, potatoes peel. We carry on.

There is a victory parade moving through the city.
The motorcade is tailed by streets of languid troops,
a marching band, batons twirling, flags, the lot.
I cannot be doing with any of it.
I scan the headlines, fold my paper, drain the cup,
go home and pack as much as I can bear.

AFTER THE FEAR WAS GONE

O the comedic pictures of the saved ones
going up like slow rockets –
the empty literalism of it!

Yet I have seen a kind of rapture:
sanderlings on a shoreline
scuttle in and out with the wash
until I'm close enough for them to clock,

so the near ones take flight,
followed by the next, then next, and on
until birds stipple the whole sky.

Fear catches, so I lift my heels and take off too,
absurdly literal in my departure,
then others go – fishermen and sunbathers –
and on inland, through cafes and hotels,

whole sweltering suburbs rising up
in this rootless contagion
until almost everyone is gone

and those who didn't feel the fear do now,
unsure if they are damned or spared,
the earth either an empty film-set
left to rot, or a world about to be re-cast.

Suspicious of each other,
these few flightless humans shun contact,
but live like survivalists on

freezers full of roadkill,
water from the ceaseless rain,
songs from TV and a learnt-by-rote line
from the last card ever sent to them.

BLISS

New Year's Eve. We gather to give thanks.
Ten years to the day our people gave up words.
I miss some: pet-names, songs with lyrics,
jokes that aren't just slapstick.
Now *voice* is a pocket-book of symbols.
Give me a flick through yours and I can read you
from the icons you rub faint with use,
the countless times you point to *liquor, terror, sick,*
distinctive as a lisp or smoker's growl.

No *Auld Lang Syne*, just cheers and claps,
ten thousand pocket-books fluttering like fans.
Electronic billboards flash above us,
brand-names gone, just picture after picture.
Even before the peace-law we lost faith in letters.
Midnight. I point to *wine*, I point to *want*,
I point across the square to my hotel.
You point to *cold*, you point to *home*.
I kiss you on the cheek and almost utter.

Back in my room, I hit the mini-bar,
lip-read old romances on the Pay TV,
thumb through my pocket-book to take stock
of another year in this, our silent paradise.
I notice how pristine my lists of VALUES are,
each tagged in red with an inverted cone
to warn the user this is neither act nor matter.
I point to signs for *joyful, love, sincere.*
It feels like firing blanks to me.

At times when a line from a nursery rhyme
starts to swell in my throat,
it pays to recall how words failed us

– war graves, massacres, neighbour on neighbour –
how the lag between speech and object
let in propaganda, slant-reads, mistranslations.
So the price of hope is wordlessness. Needless to say,
some nights I ache to shout the house down.
All this is spoken only in my head.

A MANCUNIAN TAXI-DRIVER
FORESEES HIS DEATH

On a radio show some self-help guru says
the earth will burn out in a hundred years
so treat each day as an eternity.

I am in a taxi when I hear this news,
airport-bound on the flyover
with my home town spread like a map below.

So my driver slams his foot to the floor,
and tells me that when the oil runs out
he will ship this cab to Arizona,

find the last fill-up on the planet,
drain the pump and power out into the wilderness
until the car coughs, then abandon it.

He will take from the dash this shot of his daughters,
his shark's tooth on its chain,
then leave the radio with an audience

of skulls and vultures. I wind the window down
to catch my breath and ask *what kind
of funeral is that?* Then him: *It's just a made-up one.*

He drops me by the long-haul sign
and I give him a tip well over the odds.
As I stand with my bags it begins to rain.

A man smiles down from a floodlit billboard
– well-insured, invested, sound –
which leaves me feeling heartsore, undefended.

AMERICAN PIT BULL

Heredity presents this terrier,
hard-bred to go for the throat,
caged in the unclaimed baggage area
of Terminal Two in August heat.
Foursquare, primed, withheld,
his eyes flick as I kneel to talk:
Hey, boy. Who flies you round the world
then leaves you in the sun to cook?
And though his denouement will come
in some dank warehouse with a mob,
he looks at me and has my sum:
dumb creature doesn't know his job.
With every step, his blood-line
served to bind him to his purpose,
as with each succession mine
has cut me further loose.
His path is clear - to wait, then kill.
But elsewhere due to admin error
pacing the wrong terminal,
his boss bemoans the war on terror,
how guys in caps with paranoia
choose to make dogs disappear.

THE IMMORTALITY OF THE CRAB

The clearest thought, it came like this:
flat out on a flop-house bed

a million miles from commonplace,
cocooned in my mosquito net,

a would-be war reporter sent too late
to some shit-hole ceasefire city,

bussed in through parties in the streets,
and missing you already.

No cash for drink, no work to do,
I lay and watched the ceiling fan

a seed-head like the ones we blew
to find out who loved who, and when

the power failed, it slowed until
its blades came clear

and in the darkness it was animal;
a starfish, then a spider,

then at last a crab appeared.
It took the gift of its own weight,

fell still, and in the street below I heard
a moment of pure respite –

billboards blanked, traffic stopped,
cellar bars turned crypt, breath held.

And so this vision – ice-cold – dropped
into my head, or rather, scuttled.

Yes, it had to do with death,
but smacked of liberation, not despair,

a fixed point in the ocean depths,
an anchor *in extremis* where

ghost creatures feed on whale-fall,
where the sea is all, and all-in-all.

Whenever I'm lost I go there still.

MANUMISSION

Not a slow dissolution of salt into water,
a folding down of dead leaves into earth,
a curl and ink-out smoke of letters in a fire,
a rise and gone of breath in open air,

but an awakening in skin so real it hurts,
a stretch and flex and flinch under a sun that burns,
a rain that makes us blink and spit,
in clothes like none we knew but all a perfect

fit and our city rebuilt brick by brick so
hard it casts the old place as a ghost, so we
tread the streets to trace the ones we love
and find them all, remade but recognisable,

take them in our arms, kiss them, hold them
fast as if we fear to lose them all again
but never will, which is the scandal of it,
the refusal to deliver a denouement.

NOTES & ACKNOWLEDGEMENTS

Epigraphs

The Wilde line comes from *The Soul of Man Under Socialism*. Tom Stoppard's line is from *Arcadia*. Beryl Bainbridge's line is from *English Journey*, with thanks to Jonathan Schofield, whose guide *Manchester* made me aware of BB's quotation.

Great Northern Diver

Black Poplars, also known as Manchester Poplars, are a tree native to the city, adapted to live through the pollution of the industrial revolution.

Superintendent of Public Spectacles

The composer Donizetti was called to appear before an official with this title in Palermo in 1825 to account for a disastrous opening night.

Manuka

The opening line 'deliver [us] from blood, O God' is from the Douay–Rheims translation of *Psalm 51*, though the original translation has 'me' not 'us'.

Manchuria

The peppered moth evolved rapidly during the industrial revolution to blend in with Manchester's blackened chimneys.

Tightrope Song

Rudyard Lake in Staffordshire was a day-trip destination for Manchester mill-workers in the 19th century. The legendary tightrope-walker Carlos Trower (known as 'The African Blondin') crossed the lake in 1864 and again in 1878, drawing huge crowds. The epigraph from *Dream of the Rood* is taken from Michael Alexander's translation.

Gallery of Deleted Portraits

Responds in part to a video montage – *Bliss* – by the Mancunian artist Mishka Henner.

What's Yours Is Mine

The epigraph from Thomas More's *Utopia* uses Dominic Baker Smith's Penguin Classics edition.

Peacemaker

Commissioned for *On Shakespeare's Sonnets* (Bloomsbury) in response to Shakespeare's sonnet 35.

Course of the Anyder

The Anyder was the name (from Greek 'waterless') of the river running through the city of Amaurot in More's *Utopia*.

The Flourish

This posthumous awakening of genes was reported in the *New Scientist*, based on research at the University of Washington, Seattle.

Miss Molasses

Takes its shape and the first line of each stanza from Elizabeth Bishop's poem *The Man-Moth*. It was commissioned by Radio 3's 'The Verb' in honour of the opening of Media City at the former Salford Docks where my grandfather worked.

Bliss

The semiotician Charles Bliss (1897–1985) developed a writing system based on symbols. It was a utopian vision, based on his belief that conflict and evil were rooted in the potential of words for mistranslation and misappropriation.

The Immortality of the Crab

'*Pensar en la inmortalidad del cangrejo*' is a Spanish expression meaning 'to daydream'.

Poems in this collection have been published by or in association with:

BBC Radio 3, *BBC Radio 4*, *Bristol Festival of Ideas*, *Economist*, *FilmPoem*, *Guardian*, *Irish Times*, *Jubilee Lines* (Faber), *Just So Festival*, *Little Star*, *London Review of Books*, *Manchester Review*, *On Shakespeare's Sonnets* (Bloomsbury), *Off The Shelf* (Picador), *Poetry Ireland Review*, *Poetry London*, *PN Review*, *Prac Crit*, *Regent's Park College Oxford*, *Somerset House*.

My thanks to: Robin Robertson, Carol Ann Duffy, Andrew Kelly, Hannah Crawforth and Elizabeth Scott-Baumann, Paul Fiddes, Maggie Fergusson, Anna Webber, Faith Lawrence, Susan Roberts, Jonathan Reekie, Sarah Bird, Jeremy Grange.